The Magic Money Myth

A Guide to Banking

Published by The Socialist Party of Great Britain

52 Clapham High Street

London SW4 7UN

January 2019

ISBN 978-1-909891-17-3

Contents

INTRODUCTION

Since the Crash of 2008, blamed rightly or wrongly on the banks, there has been a renewed interest in how the banking system works, and not just among regulators. At the Occupy camps that sprang up in 2011 this was a major topic of discussion as those there looked for an alternative to capitalism, at least in its present form. Leaflets circulated reviving money theories of yesteryear and criticising 'fractional reserve banking'. The Green Party too discussed the matter and committed itself on paper to the theory that banks can create money out of thin air. Money theories and denunciations of 'banksters' are all over the internet and get a hearing from those trying to understand why the present economic system doesn't work in the interest of the majority.

Some of these theories are just plain wrong, factually mistaken about what banks do and can do. All assume that banking or monetary reform can improve the position of the majority class of wage and salary workers. But it can't as these problems arise from the capitalist system of minority ownership of the means of life and production for the market and profit rather than to meet people's needs. Monetary reform is a red herring sending in the wrong direction people who are looking for a way out of capitalism. If implemented it would not solve the problems that the majority face as it leaves their cause unchanged.

In this pamphlet we set out, as part of explaining how the capitalist economic system works, to expose factual errors about what banking is and how banks work. There is nothing especially bad about banks compared with other profit-seeking capitalist enterprises. They are merely in a different line of business. Banks are not the cause of the problems that the majority class face. It's capitalism and its production for profit. The way-out is not to reform banks or the monetary system but to abolish capitalism and replace it with a socialist society based on the common ownership and democratic control of the means of production. There would then be production directly to meet people's needs and distribution in accordance with the principle "from each according to their ability, to each according to their needs," and banks and money would be redundant.

The Socialist Party

1. CAPITALISM AND MONEY

We are living under capitalism, where the means for producing and distributing wealth (land, factories, power stations, offices, media, railways, and the like) are owned and controlled by a small fraction of the members of society. As a class this minority monopolises these means and uses them to produce wealth for sale on a market with a view to profit.

In any society wealth (all the things that are useful for human life) is newly produced by humans applying their mental and physical energies to fashion or refashion materials that originally came from nature. Under capitalism this productive work is carried out by those excluded from ownership of means of production and who, to live, are obliged to sell their mental and physical energies to an employer in return for a wage. What they produce belongs to the business that employs them and has a greater value than that of the working skills they sold to their employer and for which they were paid a wage. The difference is the source of the profit which is the aim of production.

Because, under capitalism, production is for sale, the system needs a medium of exchange, something that can be used to buy anything and which sellers will accept in return for what they are selling, something that can be exchanged for anything and everything. In a word, money.

We need not go here into the origin and evolution of money in detail. Suffice it to say that originally money was itself a product of human labour, having its own intrinsic value, which could be exchanged for any other product of labour of equal value; a role fulfilled by the precious metals gold and silver. Later, as capitalist production spread and more and more products became subject to buying and selling, governments introduced paper notes, convertible on demand into a fixed amount of gold or silver. These notes circulated alongside gold and/or silver coins. Today, the currency is composed of paper notes (and metallic tokens for smaller transactions), issued by the state or its central bank, but which are no longer convertible into gold. What in the United States is called "fiat money" from the Latin word for "let it become" as it comes into being and circulates at the will of the state.

Previously, when gold coins and paper notes convertible into gold circulated, the amount of money in circulation was more or less automatically regulated to meet the needs of the economy, not just for buying and selling but also for settling debts and paying taxes. When production and trade were expanding gold was minted into coins; when they were contracting gold coins were reconverted into gold bars. With an inconvertible paper currency, however, the government and its central bank have to estimate how much the economy needs at any time. Fiat money has to be managed.

This does not alter the fact that the need for money originates in the real, productive sector of economy. The profit that is sought is a monetary profit and the wages of the producers are paid in money. These incomes are generated in production and reflect the shares in newly produced wealth, respectively, of the owners and of the producers. In other words, it is production that generates the purchasing power to buy the new products.

However, there is no need for all of this "purchasing power" to be represented by an equivalent amount of money. This is because, although fiat money is essentially a multi- purpose voucher that can be exchanged for anything, it differs from a gift voucher or an admission ticket in that, unlike them, it is not cancelled after use but can be used again by the seller. It circulates and can be used to carry out a number of transactions. The average number is these is a measure of money's "velocity of circulation".

The amount of money needed is further reduced by the use of cheques, now themselves being replaced by bank transfers, bank cards and contactless payments. So much so that some envisage the coming of a "cashless society". It probably won't happen but cash payments as a percentage of all payments are steadily decreasing.

Banks are not part of the real economy – they don't produce any new wealth – but they do play a key role in the capitalist economy. Basically, they are financial intermediaries, accepting money originally generated in production from business and individuals who don't want to spend it immediately (but to "save" and spend later) and lending most of this to fund some business project or purchase. The role of banks under capitalism is to ensure that as little as possible of the purchasing power generated in production remains idle.

2. HOW BANKS OPERATE

Banks are profit-seeking capitalist businesses. Their business model is generating an income from the difference between the rate of interest (if any) they pay to "savers" and the higher rate they charge those they lend to. After paying their running costs, including the wages of their employees, what is left is their profit.

Here is how an online dictionary of financial terms (intended for investors who will want to know facts) describes a bank's financial model:

> "Banks take deposits from savers and pay interest on some of these accounts. They pass these funds on to borrowers and receive interest on the loans. Their profits are derived from the spread between the rate they pay for funds and the rate they receive from borrowers. The ability to pool deposits from many sources that can be lent to many different borrowers creates the flow of funds inherent in the banking system. By managing this flow of funds, banks generate profits, acting as the intermediary of interest paid and interest received, and taking the risk of offering credit".
>
> (www.yahoo.com/news/analyzing-banks-financial-statements-194222578.html)

This can be confirmed by looking at a bank's accounts. A good example is the Nationwide Building Society (a building society is a type of bank) whose 2016 *Strategic and Financial Review* booklet sent to members included an easy-to-follow diagram of their business model (reproduced on the following page).

One point to note immediately is that its funds don't come exclusively from "customer deposits" but from these plus "wholesale funding". This latter is money obtained by borrowing from the money market, i.e., from other banks and financial institutions. Customer deposits are also in effect (and in law) loans – from the depositor to the banks even if no interest is paid on some of them. Such deposits are also described by bankers as "retail" borrowing as opposed to the "wholesale" borrowing from the money market. Banks can also use their own capital to fund their lending.

This point is important because it shows that what banks lend does not have to come just from individual savers, as is sometimes suggested by critics of the view that banks are financial intermediaries.

Borrowing from the money market to relend is more risky than obtaining deposits as it is mainly in the form of short-term, renewable loans, the rate of interest over which banks have no control. It was being caught out by a sudden rise in interest rates on their wholesale borrowing that sunk Northern Rock and HBOS during the financial crash of 2008. They had relied too much on obtaining funds to relend from this source and found that, when interest rates on them suddenly rose, they were not in a position to renew them as the interest they would have had to pay was higher than the interest they were receiving from their own loans, i.e. that their "net interest income" was negative. So, not only were they not making a profit but they were not covering all of their running costs.

Strategic review

Our approach to providing financial services is straightforward - we offer a broad range of competitive mortgages, savings, current accounts and other financial products, delivering consistently excellent service to our members, who are also our owners

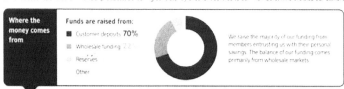

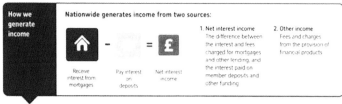

There is a measure of the extent to which banks rely, as a source of funds to relend, on wholesale compared with retail funding – the "loan-to-deposit" ratio:

> "*This measure indicates the proportion of loans that are backed by deposits rather than wholesale funding, interbank borrowing, or the proceeds of bond issuance. Most small banks and building societies operate on a loan-to-deposit ratio of under 100: Kingdom Bank, for example, says its target ratio is 95 per cent. It will not "lend out" more than 95 per cent of the total amount of deposits on its books. We would regard that as a prudent approach to lending. But the majority of large banks have far higher loan-to- deposit ratios. At the time of the financial crisis, the average ratio in UK banks was 137 per cent.*" (*City A.M.*, 5 February 2013)

As Wikipedia points out in its entry on the ratio, one of more than 100 means that "the bank borrowed money which it reloaned at higher rates, rather than relying entirely on its own deposits." (en.wikipedia.org/wiki/Loan-deposit_ratio)

Further confirmation, then, that banks don't need to rely entirely on deposits to fund their lending; they can also have recourse to borrowing from the money market.

The Nationwide diagram is a model and so did not include any figures, but these were given elsewhere in the booklet. These showed that in 2016 deposits and borrowings amounted to £204,546 million while loans were £178,807 million. "Liquid reserves" – cash, reserves deposited with the Bank of England, and short-term bonds that can be quickly converted into cash – were £23,000 million.

As deposits were £138,715 million its loan-to-deposit ratio in 2016 was 128.9, which means that 22.5 percent of its lending was funded by money-market borrowing. Its liquidity (to loans) ratio, which we shall meet again when it comes to discussing "fractional reserve banking", was 12.9 percent.

The other thing to note about a bank's accounts is that, like all capitalist businesses, they are set out in accordance with the principle of double-entry bookkeeping, with every "asset" acquired being balanced by a corresponding "liability" and every "liability" incurred being balanced by a corresponding "asset".

Thus, when someone makes a deposit (it could just be the payment in of their salary) the money paid in is recorded as an "asset"; the corresponding "liability" is an IOU from the bank to the depositor. The same applies in the case of wholesale borrowing by the bank: the money borrowed is an asset, with the liability being the obligation to repay it. When a bank makes a loan, it is the other way round. The money loaned is recorded as a "liability" – the bank has handed it over to the borrower to spend, so it no longer belongs to the bank – with the corresponding "asset" being an IOU from the borrower to the bank. This bookkeeping practice is, as we shall see, frequently misunderstood as meaning that when a bank makes a loan it is literally creating a new real asset, in the non-financial sense of something useful or valuable, that did not exist before.

To complete the picture, in 2016 Nationwide's net interest income was £3,086 million, other income and gains were £386 million. Administrative expenses were £1,847 million and various provisions £246 million. The result for the year was therefore a profit of £1,279 million.

We are now in a position to examine the various claims that banks have the ability to create money to lend out of nothing, i.e. without needing funds obtained from depositors, the money market or their own reserves. We can test these claims against the example just given of the model and finances of a typical bank.

3. THE NEW THEORY OF MONEY

That banks are financial intermediaries borrowing at one rate of interest and lending at another, higher rate was relatively clear and generally accepted until the 1920s and 1930s when the definition of "money" came to be changed.

Previously, money had been defined as the currency, as notes and coins, cash. During this period its definition was extended to include what had previously been called "bank credit" on the ostensibly plausible ground that this too affected spending. Governments were interested in how much banks were lending, both to manage fiat money and to control total spending as part of their attempt to control the operation of the capitalist economy. Controlling bank lending was one of the ways in which they sought to do this.

Money and the money supply are now defined, both in textbooks and financial regulations, as including bank deposits.

There's M0, M1, M2, M3 and M4. The two most used are probably M0 and M4. M0 is notes and coins + banks' reserves at the Bank of England (Basic, or Narrow, money). M4 is this + the amount held in the current and savings accounts of banks and building societies (Broad money).

M4 is many times M0. According to a Bank of England publication:

> "*Broad money is made up of bank deposits – which are essentially IOUs from commercial banks to households and companies – and currency – mostly IOUs from the central bank. Of the two types of broad money, bank deposits make up the vast majority – 97% of the amount currently in circulation. And in the modern economy, those bank deposits are mostly created by commercial banks themselves.*" ("Money Creation in the Modern Economy", *Bank of England Quarterly Bulletin*, 2014, Q1)

The statement that "bank deposits are mostly created by commercial banks themselves" is misleading to the point of being untrue. It has been taken by opponents of the "intermediary" theory of banking as meaning that banks "create" money in the same sort of way as states now create currency – by a simple administrative decision. As the state does create currency "out of nothing" in this way, so some think that banks create money in the same way; that banks, too, can create in effect fiat money and that they actually do this whenever they make a loan. This is the money-creationist theory of banking, which might also be called the thin-air theory. It has also been called the mystical theory of banking.

If you define bank loans – what used to be called bank credit – as money, then, by definition, banks "create money" whenever they make a loan; they are one and the same thing. However, it does not follow that what banks are lending has been "created" by them in the sense that it did not exist previously. What banks are doing when they make a loan is indeed adding to spending, but this is not done by creating new purchasing power; it is by activating purchasing power that would otherwise remain idle, through lending it to be spent. Even if you accept the modern theory of money, it makes more sense to say that banks "activate money" when they make a loan rather than "creating" it.

Aside from the ambiguity arising from the use of the word "create", the statement in the Bank of England's publication is inconsistent on its own terms. It says that bank deposits are *"essentially IOUs from commercial banks to households and companies"* and that they *"are mostly created by commercial banks themselves"*.

In a sense bank deposits could be said to be IOUs, but there are two kinds of bank deposits depending on how the money got there. If it was paid in by a bank customer it is recorded, according to the principles of double-entry bookkeeping, as an "asset" with the corresponding "liability" being an IOU *from* the bank to the depositor. If, on the other hand, it has been credited to the customer's account as a loan from the bank it is the other way round, the "liability" is the money in the account (it no longer belongs to the bank) and the corresponding "asset" is the IOU *to* the bank from the borrower.

Logically, then, even on the modern definition of money, only the second type of bank deposit could meaningfully be said to have been "created" by the bank in the sense of being due to an action initiated by the bank itself. Since some of what banks lend comes from what has been deposited with them, to include both kinds of deposit as money involves some double-counting.

Even if the figures are adjusted to take account of this double-counting, it is still the case that bank loans are many times greater than state fiat money. But there is nothing extraordinary about this. Since state fiat money circulates and its use is being economised by electronic transfers and bank cards it is what you would expect. It is no more amazing or alarming than that the amount of fiat money in existence is only a small percentage of the total prices of what's for sale.

4. THE PURE 'THIN AIR' THEORY OF BANKING

If an article in a prestigious Bank of England publication expresses itself inconsistently it can be expected that money-creationists will get it even more wrong.

Here are a couple of examples, taken from leaflets distributed at the Occupy Camp outside St. Paul's in London in December 2011:

> "Banks do not lend anything. They create money as credit out of nothing [when they "lend"] and charge interest on something which costs nothing to produce."

> "The numbers in your bank account were all created, essentially out of nothing, not by the Bank of England or the Royal Mint, but by commercial banks . . . Rather than taking money from a saver and lending it to a borrower (as per the common understanding of banking), they simply write new numbers into the bank account of a borrower – effectively creating new money."

And you thought that when you had your wage or salary paid into your account this represented what you had earned by working!

It is not just distributors of photocopied leaflets who hold this view. An attempt to lend some academic credibility to the theory that banks create money to lend out of nothing has been made by Professor Richard Werner, then of Southampton University's Business School. In 2014 he published a paper entitled "Can banks individually create money out of nothing? – The theories and the empirical evidence" (widely available on the internet and widely cited by money-creationists). On 7 August 2013 he filmed exactly what happened when, as part of an empirical study, a small savings bank in Bavaria made him a loan of €200,000. He observed that at no point did the bank employee responsible for authorising loans check if deposits or reserves were sufficient to pay the loan and that no money was transferred from one department of the bank to another. He also observed (and photographed) that both the bank's assets and liabilities, and so its balance sheet, were recorded as having increased by €200,000. He, rather modestly, drew the conclusion:

> "Thus it can now been said with confidence for the first time – possibly in the 5,000 years' history of banking – that it has been empirically demonstrated that each individual bank creates credit and money out of nothing, when it extends what is called a 'bank loan'. The bank does not loan any existing money, but instead creates new money. The money supply is created as 'fairy dust' produced by the banks out of thin air."

He had demonstrated nothing of the kind, only that the bank, like all banks, practised double-entry bookkeeping. He did not theorise on how a banker might have recorded a loan in the 3,000 years before this was practised. Nor what would have happened if the employee had authorised a loan of more than the bank's reserves or than what it had had deposited with it. Above all, he did not record what happened the following day when he says the €200,000 was transferred to another bank. He promised a follow-up paper on this but this does not seem to have been published, perhaps because it would have refuted his theory as the bank's reserves would then have been reduced by €200,000 and so recorded. If the loan had been greater than the bank's reserves such a transfer would not – could not – have gone through.

5. FRACTIONAL RESERVE BANKING

Professor Werner appears to be of the view that an individual bank does not need any reserves at all to make a loan. Others don't go that far. For instance, on 15 October 2008 the *Times* published a letter by a Malcolm Parkin which began:

> "*Sir, only 3 per cent of money exists as cash. Therefore the rest is magic money conjured into existence, and issued as debt by banks, at a ratio of about 33 magic pounds to 1 real pound, by the quite legal means of fractional reserve banking.*"

Quite apart from the "therefore" being an invalid deduction, this is to completely misunderstand fractional reserve banking.

When a bank receives a deposit it retains a "fraction" as cash to deal with any withdrawals in cash; the rest is available for lending. Bankers learn from experience what fraction is safe. In the United States banks are legally obliged to retain as cash 10 percent of some kinds of deposit. In Britain it used to be 8 percent but now there is no laid down "cash ratio", not even the 3 percent Malcolm Parkin assumes. Banks are, however, required to keep an agreed minimum amount with the Bank of England.

If the cash ratio is 10 percent what this means is that, for every £100 deposited, a bank retains £10, leaving the remaining £90 available for lending. This is frequently misunderstood as meaning that for every £100 deposited a bank can lend out £900 "conjured into existence" out of nothing. And not only by leaflet distributors and "Disgusted" of Tunbridge Wells but by Professor Werner too.

In a Youtube talk on "Banking & the Economy" he declares:

> "*Somewhat stylized and applied to a standard fractional reserve system, the process works as follows. When Bank A receives a new deposit of £100 and a 1% reserve requirement is applied by the central bank, the bank will not deposit £1 with the central bank and lend £99 to borrowers (as many textbooks state), but instead deposit the entire 100 with the central bank, thus being able to extend credit amounting to £9,900.*"
> (www.youtube.com/watch?v=wDHSUgA29Ls)

The very absurdity of this conclusion shows that the theory cannot be correct.

Fractional reserve banking, properly understood, is what banking is all about: taking in money, retaining a minimum as cash, and lending out the rest. If a bank had to retain as cash all the money deposited with it, it would not be a bank. It would be a glorified safety deposit box.

One theory of the origin of modern banking is that it started with goldsmiths in London in the middle of the seventeenth century who did begin to lend out money deposited with them for safe- keeping. Richard Cantillon in his *Essay on the Nature of Trade in General*, written in 1730, described their practice:

> *"If a hundred economical gentlemen or Proprietors of Land, who put by every year money from their savings to buy Land on occasion, deposit each one 10,000 ounces of silver with a Goldsmith or Banker in London, to avoid the trouble of keeping this money in their houses and the thefts which might be made of it, they will take from them notes payable on demand. Often they will leave their money there a long time, and even when they have made some purchase they will give notice to the Banker some time in advance to have their money ready when the formalities and legal documents are complete.*
>
> *In these circumstances the Banker will often be able to lend 90,000 ounces of the 100,000 he owes throughout the year and will only need to keep in hand 10,000 ounces to meet all the withdrawals. He has to do with wealthy and economical persons; as fast as one thousand ounces are demanded of him in one direction, a thousand are brought to him from another. It is enough as a rule for him to keep in hand the tenth part of his deposits. There have been examples and experiences of this in London. Instead of the individuals in question keeping in hand all the year round the greatest part of 100,000 ounces the custom of depositing it with a banker causes 90,000 ounces of the 100,000 to be put into circulation."*

There is no question here of the goldsmith-bankers issuing "notes payable on demand" of 900,000 ounces of silver. Despite this, there is a cartoon-style film on the internet, *Money as Debt* by Paul Grignon, which, besides suggesting that there were goldsmith-bankers in every town at the end of the Middle Ages (whereas they only existed in the seventeenth and eighteenth centuries in the commercial centre that London was), claims that in the end the goldsmiths began to lend out the whole of what had been deposited with them and even to issue receipts, which circulated as means of payment, for more than the money deposited. This would have been imprudent, indeed completely reckless, as the slightest hint that a goldsmith-banker might be unable to honour his receipts would lead to a rush to withdraw money and ruin him. It would also be unlawful and lead to the goldsmith languishing in a debtor's jail. In any event, there is no evidence that any of them did this or even considered doing it. It's just fake history.

At one time academic economics tried to rescue the claim that banks could lend more than had originally been deposited with them by maintaining that, while an individual bank could not do this, all banks together (and by implication a single bank on its own) could. This was elaborated as a theoretical justification of the policy that governments were pursuing at the time of trying to control bank lending by varying the cash ratio they required banks to maintain.

In chapter 16 of the 1961 edition of his widely-used textbook *Economics*, Nobel Prize winner Paul Samuelson wrote:

> "We now turn to one of the most interesting aspects of money and credit, the process called 'multiple expansion of bank deposits'. Most people have heard that in some mysterious manner banks can create money out of thin air, but few really understand how the process works.
>
> Actually, there is nothing magical or incomprehensible about the creation of bank deposits. At every step of the way, one can follow what is happening to the banks' accounts. The true explanation of deposit creation is simple.
>
> What is hard to grasp are the false explanations that still circulate.
>
> According to these false explanations, the managers of an ordinary bank are able, by some use of their fountain pens, to lend several dollars for each dollar deposited with them. No wonder practical bankers see red when such power is attributed to them. They only wish they could do so. As every banker knows, he cannot invest money that he does not have; and money that he invests in buying a security or making a loan soon leaves his bank.
>
> Bankers, therefore, often go to the opposite extreme. They sometimes argue that the banking system cannot (and does not) create money; 'After all', they say, 'we can invest only what is left with us. We don't create anything. We only put the community's savings to work.' Bankers who argue in this way are quite wrong. They have become enmeshed in our old friend, the fallacy of composition: what is true for each is not thereby true for all. The banking system as a whole can do what each small bank cannot do: it can expand its loans and investments many times the original cash given it, but meanwhile each small bank is lending out only a fraction of its deposits."

He assumed a cash ratio of 20 percent which meant that a bank had to hold $2 out of every $10 deposited with it. In his example someone initially deposits $1000 in a bank. That bank retains $200 as cash and lends out $800. The borrowers spend this and it eventually, via those who they buy from, finds its way to one or other bank in the system as different amounts in different banks totalling $800. Twenty percent of this -- $160 -- is retained as cash and $640 lent out. This, too, returns to the banking system and 80 percent of it is loaned out. The process goes on

> "until, supposing that there are no leaks and no bank keeps reserves of over 20%, the end of the process will be that all the banks in the banking system will have loaned out 5 times the original deposit, i.e. $5000."

17

This doesn't really help the money-creationists because Samuelson was adamant that no individual bank can "jack its deposit to five times its cash reserves" and that "it cannot lend or invest more than it has received from depositors". So, their basic claim is denied. However, in suggesting that the whole banking system (or a single bank) could "create money out of thin air" he was lending credibility, if only by the language he used, to the thin-air theory of banking. His theoretical model is not mathematically wrong, just unrealistic and misleading.

What it overlooks is that, while at the end of the process the total amount loaned out is indeed $5000, the total number of deposits has been $6000. No extra money has been created. All that has happened in this textbook construction is that the money originally deposited (whose appearance is not explained but which can only have come out of previously produced wealth) has circulated and been used to make deposits totalling $6000. In fact, Samuelson himself conceded this when he wrote that "the banking system *and the public* do, between them, create about $5 of bank deposits for each new dollar of reserves that comes to the banks." (our emphasis). So it is not a question of all banks together on their own creating money from thin air to lend. All of what they lent was deposited by "the public". His practical bankers were right after all to say "we invest only what is left with us. We don't create anything".

6. LOANS NEED TO BE FUNDED

Other, more subtle versions of the thin-air theory of banking argue that, while neither a single bank nor all banks together can create from nothing money to lend, the banking system centred around the central bank can. Since the central bank can create money at will such versions are not inherently incoherent. However, it is the language in which these versions are expressed that is a problem as it can be seized on by the advocates of cruder versions of the thin-air theory to justify their version.

For instance, David Graeber, author of *Debt: The First 5000 Years*, has argued:

> "There's really no limit on how much banks can create, provided they can find someone willing to borrow it. They will never get caught short, for the simple reason that borrowers do not, generally speaking, take the cash and put it under their mattresses; ultimately any money a bank loans out will just end up in some bank again. What's more, insofar as banks do need to acquire funds from the central bank, they can borrow as much as they like." ("The truth is out: money is just an IOU, and the banks are rolling in it", Guardian, 18 March, 2014.)

This is a variation of Samuelson's "multiple deposit creation" model and no more shows that the banking system can create money to lend out of nothing than does his. What keeps the lending going is that the sum of money keeps getting re-deposited into the system. In other words, the loans are matched by deposits from "the public".

Graeber was commenting on the article "Money creation in the modern economy", already discussed, that appeared in the *Bank of England Quarterly Bulletin* in 2014. Latching on to a statement in it that "rather than banks receiving deposits when households save and then lending them out, bank lending creates deposits", he remarked:

> "Just consider what might happen if mortgage holders realised the money the bank lent them is not, really, the life savings of some thrifty pensioner, but something the bank just whisked into existence through its possession of a magic wand which we, the public handed over to it."

When the article says "bank lending creates deposits" it was referring to the double-entry bookkeeping practice of recording balancing new liabilities with a new asset and vice versa. Graeber's interpretation is given some support as the article does say that when this is done "new money is created", adding:

> "For this reason, some economists have referred to bank deposits as 'fountain pen money', created at the stroke of bankers' pens when they approve loans."

Approving a loan and how it is recorded in a bank's books is of some interest (though hardly worth filming as Professor Werner did), but why stop at this bookkeeping stage as this is only the beginning of the process? What happens next – when the borrower spends the money that bank has put in their account as the amount of the loan – is also important, in fact more important.

When, later in the article, the authors do go into the details of what happens when a bank makes a new loan, they explicitly state that the amount of the loan does have to be funded:

> "*Suppose an individual bank lowers the rate it charges on its loans, and that attracts a household to take out a mortgage. The moment the mortgage loan is made, the household's account is credited with new deposits. And once they purchase the house, they pass their deposits on to the house seller . . . The buyer's bank would then have fewer deposits than assets. **In the first instance, the buyer's bank settles with the seller's bank by transferring reserves.***" (Our emphasis)

What are these "reserves"? They are what the bank has deposited at the Bank of England. This will have come, not from thin air, but either from the bank's own capital or even from money deposited with it by savers. Either way, it will be previously existing money. What happens is that some of the lending bank's reserves with the Bank of England are transferred to those there of the seller's bank.

The authors go on (remember that by "liabilities" they mean the IOUs from the bank to those it gets money from):

> "*if a given bank financed all of its new loans in this way, it would soon run out of reserves. Banks therefore try to attract or retain additional liabilities to accompany their new loans . . . By attracting new deposits, the bank can increase its lending without running down its reserves.*"

Deposits that will come from, among others, "the life savings of some thrifty pensioner".

Banks can also have recourse to the money market but, one way or the other, must acquire the funds to cover their loans:

> "*Alternatively, a bank can borrow from other banks or attract other forms of liabilities, at least temporarily. But whether through deposits or other liabilities, **the bank would need to make sure it was attracting and retaining some kind of funds to keep expanding lending.***" (authors' bold).

So, the famous Bank of England article, much referenced in the literature of the thin-air school of banking, does not say that loans don't have to be funded and can just be conjured up from nowhere by the wave of a magic wand. It says, precisely, that they *do* have to be funded.

It has to be said, though, that if the article has been misunderstood, by Graeber and others, as saying that banks create the money they lend by waving a magic wand, this is the authors' own fault. They could have made things clear by saying in a single passage that "when a bank makes a loan, this is recorded in its books as a deposit in the borrower's bank account; when the borrower spends the loan the bank has to mobilise funds to finance it". They do in fact say this if you read the article, but in the introductory overview they chose to emphasise only the first part, leaving the reader to find the second in the body of the article. The uncritical and gratuitous aside about "fountain pen money" didn't help either.

The article is clear, however, that banks are profit-seeking financial intermediaries:

> "*A bank's business model relies on receiving a higher interest rate on the loans (or other assets) than the rate it pays out on its deposits (or other liabilities) . . . The commercial bank uses the difference, or spread, between the expected return on their assets and liabilities to cover its operating costs and to make profits.*"

Which brings us back to where we started.

7. TOWARDS A CASHLESS SOCIETY?

Money performs various roles. Its primary ones are to measure the value of items of wealth produced for sale (expressed as their price) and to be the medium through which they are bought and sold (so they don't have to be exchanged directly with each other, as with barter). Money is also a means for settling debts and paying taxes and a unit of account (for calculating income and expenditure, profit and loss).

Originally money, in its primary roles, took the form of an item of wealth that had its own intrinsic value by virtue of being a product of human labour, in particular silver and gold. So, when it was used to buy something there was an exchange of items of wealth of equal value. The price of an item of wealth produced for sale was in fact originally expressed as a weight of the money commodity (in England a pound was once literally an amount of silver weighing a pound). Coins, as pieces of the money commodity stamped by the state as a guarantee of their weight, were introduced in Ancient times and made buying and selling easier.

Coins can function as money even if they don't actually contain the stamped amount of silver or gold. Even in Ancient Greece and Rome copper coins were used for small payments as tokens for the real thing. Later paper notes were too for larger payments. Notes and coins – "cash" – is still today the popular conception of what money is; they are money but only in its role as the medium of buying and selling.

Today, commodity money has been entirely replaced by fiat money, issued by the state. So now when anything is bought or sold it is no longer an exchange of items of equal value but an exchange of an item of wealth for a token of the same face-value but which itself has virtually no value (the value of the metal in a pound coin is only a few pence). The face-value of these tokens is decreed and guaranteed by the state. This works as long as the state is stable.

Coins and notes are not the only possible forms that tokens for money as a medium of buying and selling can take or in fact have taken. They were the ones that evolved historically given the technology. The Ancient Greeks could smelt and mint silver but could not have issued paper notes. That only became possible after paper-making and printing technology had reached a certain point. Today, with the development of information technology, another form has become possible, one which renders the physical handover of tokens unnecessary.

According to UK Finance, 2017 was the first year in which payments by debit card (including contactless) exceeded those by cash:

> "By the end of 2017 there were nearly 119 million contactless cards in circulation and, with customers and businesses increasingly choosing to use contactless

cards and card acceptance devices, it is anticipated 36 per cent of all payments across the UK will be contactless in 2027. As consumers increasingly turn to contactless payments in situations where previously they may have paid using cash, 2017 saw a decrease in cash payments by 15 per cent to 13.1 billion payments. Around 3.4 million consumers almost never used cash at all, instead relying on cards and other payment methods to manage their spending." (Press release 'Convenience of debit card payments puts cash in second place', 18 June 2018.)

Some see this as holding out the prospect of a "cashless society" in which there would be no physical money. This is theoretically possible but unlikely in practice. UK Finance estimated that by 2027 cash payments would still represent 16 percent of all payments, even if down from the 34 percent in 2017.

Even if all payments became electronic this would not mean that society would be moneyless. As production would still be carried on for sale with a view to profit, there would still be a medium of exchange even if not tangible (only a string of computer code in cyberspace) and there would still be a measure of value (items of wealth would still have prices).

One consequence of a cashless society would be that every single monetary transaction would be recorded, which would mean that they could be available to the state, unlike cash payments which can be anonymous.

The prospect of the state knowing everybody's finances was one reason why a group of anti- state ideologists in the US came up with the idea of devising an electronic equivalent of cash. In 2009 they published a paper 'Bitcoin: A Peer-to-Peer Electronic Cash System' which stated:

"A purely peer-to-peer version of electronic cash would allow payments to be sent directly from one party to another without going through a financial institution." (bitcoin.org/en/bitcoin-paper).

So it was not just the state but banks too that were to be by-passed, both considered responsible for mismanaging fiat money and causing financial crises.

The basis of the proposed system was to be a network of computers without a central server, all the computers being in direct contact with all the others. Hence peer-to-peer. The problem with such a decentralised, or rather, non-centralised system is how to verify that the person making the payment has not already spent the "electronic cash" attributed to them. The innovation here was to apply "blockchain" technology in which transactions are recorded electronically in a ledger that cannot be changed retroactively.

Under the scheme, when someone makes a payment, other members of the network compete to solve a complicated mathematical problem, the first to solve it being rewarded in bitcoin. This so-called bitcoin "mining" involves consuming huge amounts of electricity and computer time.

Technically a bitcoin is a voucher enabling the holder to access Bitcoin's money transfer service and whose price is entirely dependent on demand. Bitcoins didn't have a price until 2010 when it was made convertible into fiat money at the rate of 1 bitcoin = 0.003 US cents. From that year on, people who were not part of the peer-to-peer network began to buy bitcoins. The demand came from those attracted by one of the features of the system – its disguising of payers and payees – which allowed their transactions to remain anonymous in the way that cash payments could; people such as drugs barons, arms dealers, money launderers and others wanting to avoid financial regulations. This is why the bitcoin price has been described as "an index of money laundering".

Bitcoins only exist as strings of computer code, and are intrinsically worthless. But so are fiat money's notes and coins, only behind them is the state guaranteeing their face-value. There is nothing behind bitcoins. Yet in 2017 the price of a single bitcoin overtook the price of an ounce of gold and reached $19,000 in December from less than $1,000 at the beginning of the year. It has since fallen to around a third of its peak price.

It is this aspect – as an object of speculation – that has led some commentators to describe bitcoins as a "crypto-asset" rather than a "crypto-currency", something people can invest in hoping that it will hold or increase its monetary value over time. In any event, bitcoins are never going to replace fiat money, if only because states will not allow it.

There is a certain irony in the situation of one group of computer experts working out ways to render physical cash unnecessary and another group working to create an electronic equivalent of cash. From the point of view of rationally satisfying human needs, all the human ingenuity and all the computer time and resources involved in both projects is so much waste. In a socialist society, based on the common ownership of productive resources with production to satisfy people's needs, there would be no need for an electronic payments system; in fact, no need for any sort of payments system since buying and selling will have been replaced by access to products according to need – and so no need for money, not as a measure of value any more than as a medium of exchange.

8. SOCIALISM OR BANKING REFORM?

Since banks are capitalist institutions which will have no place in a socialist society, why does having a correct understanding of how they work matter? Basically, because it is part of understanding how the capitalist economic system works and how it can only work in the way it does – as a profit-making system under which there is an economic imperative that making profits should have priority over meeting people's needs adequately. It cannot be made to work in any other way, so there is no point in trying to reform it to make it serve the needs of all.

The advocates of the various rival theories of banking fall in two groups. There are those who want to show capitalist governments what they should do to better manage the capitalist economy so as to avoid financial crises and economic downturns. And those who think they have found a flaw in the monetary system (but haven't) and propose a remedy for this.

The first group are typically academics and journalists. Their basic premise is that the government can control the capitalist economic system so as to ensure steady growth; it is just a matter of pursuing the correct policy. They see capitalism as a system that is driven, not so much by the pursuit of profit but by satisfying paying demand. More lending means more spending, hence the importance they attach to controlling bank lending.

They blame the banks for causing, by lending too much, a period of economic growth to end in a financial crash. So, they propose various ways to control bank lending – varying the cash ratio or the reserves banks are required to keep with the central bank or interest rates – and elaborate banking theories to back up the particular way they favour. None has worked, basically because banks are not in control of the amount they lend. That depends on the state of the economy.

Banks cannot decide to lend more if there is no extra credit-worthy demand for loans, as is the case in an economic downturn. On the other hand, in a boom, as profit-seeking businesses themselves, they cannot forgo the chance to make a profit by lending more when there is a strong demand from businesses for capital to take advantage of an expanding market – which both businesses and banks assume will continue. The boom comes to an end, not for a monetary reason, but when one key sector overproduces in relation to the rest of the economy with the knock-on effect leading to a general economic downturn.

Some of these theories are more accurate than others about how capitalism works – for instance, those that realise that banks are financial intermediaries or that banks cannot spontaneously initiate a lending and spending boom. However, we don't take sides in their disputes as we are not concerned, as all of them are, with advising governments on the best way to try to run capitalism. As far as we are concerned, both the theory of how the capitalist economy works and the experience of governments' failed attempts to control it show that capitalism cannot be controlled. In fact, it is the other way round. Governments can do little more than react to what capitalism throws at them as it moves through the various phases of its economic cycle. Governments – and their would-be advisers – might propose, but it is capitalism that disposes.

We do, however, recognise that, while no banking reforms can avert financial crises, some can make things worse. As Karl Marx put it:

> "*Ignorant and confused banking laws, such as those of 1844-5, may intensify the monetary crisis. But no bank legislation can abolish crises themselves.*" (*Capital*, Volume 3, Chapter 30, Penguin Books edition, p. 621.)

This misunderstanding applies, with particular force, to the second group of banking theorists. Because the flaw in the banking and monetary system they think they have detected does not in fact exist, their proposals to remedy it are much more likely to make things worse rather than simply be irrelevant and harmless. Depending on the particular imagined flaw and its imaginary remedy, the result could be either too much fiat money being issued (resulting in roaring inflation) or not enough bank lending being permitted (resulting in an economic slowdown).

The second group don't tend to be academics. They are concerned about finding a solution to people's everyday problems but have got hold of the wrong end of the stick, attributing to some flaw in the banking and monetary system the problems that are in fact caused by the capitalist economic system of production for profit. In so doing they misdirect the attention of people concerned about these problems to banking and monetary reform rather than to abolishing capitalism.

Thus, for instance, one of the leaflets handed out at Occupy St. Paul's claims:

> "*We can help solve problems like debt, poverty, economic chaos and environmental breakdown just by fixing the way that money and banking works.*"

Because what they propose is based on a non-existing flaw they have been called "money cranks", defined as:

> "*A person who believes that all, or the vast majority of, social ills are caused by the current money system and thus can be solved by implementing an imaginary money system that they have designed.*"
> (leaders.economicblogs.org/gei/2017/constitutes-money-crank)

26

A bit unkind perhaps, but true and why socialists need to refute their flawed theories and proposed remedies.

As capitalism is the cause of the problems that currently face humanity in general and the majority class of wage and salary workers and their dependents in particular, the only way to provide a framework within which these problems can be lastingly solved is to get rid of capitalism.

Capitalism is based on a class monopoly of the means of production which prevents the productive forces built up under it being used to provide the plenty for all that they could. Socialism ends this by making the means of production the common property of society as a whole, no longer owned by rich individuals, corporations or the state but under the democratic control of a classless society of free men and women.

With class ownership replaced by common ownership, production can be geared to directly meeting people's needs instead of, under capitalism, for sale with a view to profit. In fact, not only not for profit but not for sale either. The question socialist society will have to deal with will no longer be to sell what has been produced but to distribute it. Services can be provided free and people will have free access in the common stores to what they need to live and enjoy life in accordance with the principle of "from each according to their ability, to each according to their needs".

With the replacement of exchange by distribution, banks will become redundant. They will cease to exist and their buildings and computers put to good use. The coloured pieces of paper, the metal tokens and the plastic cards of today can take their place alongside the coins of Ancient Rome and Greece in the Museum of Antiquities.

27

Discover more about The Socialist Party of Great Britain

Or go to this link online:

https://www.worldsocialism.org/spgb/3-free-standards

Introducing The Socialist Party

The Socialist Party advocates a society where production is freed from the artificial constraints of profit and organised for the benefit of all on the basis of material abundance. It does not have policies to ameliorate aspects of the existing social system.

The *Socialist Standard* is the combative monthly journal of the Socialist Party of Great Britain, published without interruption since 1904 and infuriating and exasperating political opponents in equal measure. The journal was placed on a list of publications banned for export during World War I for its call for workers not to fight for their countries, and in World War II it evaded the censor largely by producing articles on ancient wars as cover for the Party's implacable opposition to the conflict.

In the 1930s the *Socialist Standard* explained why capitalism would not collapse of its own accord, in response to widespread claims to the contrary, and continues to hold this view in face of the notion's recent popularity. Beveridge's welfare measures of the 1940s were viewed as a reorganisation of poverty and a necessary 'expense' of production, and Keynesian policies designed to overcome slumps an illusion. Today, the journal exposes as false the view that banks create money out of thin air, and explains why actions to prevent the depredation of the natural world can have limited effect and run counter to the nature of capitalism itself.

Gradualist reformers like the Labour Party believed that capitalism could be transformed through a series of social measures, but have merely become routine managers of the system. The Bolsheviks had to be content with developing Russian capitalism under a one-party dictatorship. Both failures have given socialism a quite different – and unattractive -- meaning: state ownership and control. As the *Socialist Standard* pointed out before both courses were followed, the results would more properly be called state capitalism.

The Socialist Party is not a left-wing organisation nor its journal a left-wing journal. 'Left-wing' has simply become an umbrella designation for parties and organisations demanding modifications to how we now live. The Party and the World Socialist Movement affirm that capitalism is incapable of meaningful change in the interests of the majority; that the basis of exploitation is the wages/money system. The *Socialist Standard* is proud to have kept alive the original idea of what socialism is -- a classless, stateless, wageless, moneyless society or, defined positively, a democracy in which free and equal men and women co-operate to produce the things they need to live and enjoy life, to which they have free access in accordance with the principle 'from each according to their abilities, to each according to their needs'.

The Socialist Party, 52 Clapham High Street, London SW4 7UN

Tel: 020 7622 3811 Text: 07732 831192

spgb@worldsocialism.org   spgb.net

The Companion Parties of Socialism

Socialist Party of Canada/Parti Socialiste du Canada
Box 31024, Victoria B.C. V8N 6J3 Canada.
Email: spc@worldsocialism.org

World Socialist Party (India)
257 Baghajatin 'E' Block (East), Kolkata -
700086 Tel: 033-2425-0208
Email: wspindia@hotmail.com

World Socialist Party (New Zealand)
P.O. Box 1929, Auckland, NI, New Zealand.

World Socialist Party of the United States
P.O. Box 440247, Boston, MA 02144 USA.
Email: boston@wspus.org

EUROPE

Ireland:
Cork: Kevin Cronin, 5 Curragh Woods, Frankfield, T12 KHN2
Tel: 021 4896427
Newtownabbey: Nigel McCullough, Tel: 028 90852062

Denmark: Graham Taylor, Kjaerslund 9, Floor 2 (middle), DK-8260 Viby J.

Germany: Norbert. Email: weltsozialismus@gmx.net

Italy: Gian Maria Freddi, Via Polano n. 137, 371142 Verona

Norway: Robert Stafford, Email: hallblithe@yahoo.com

Spain: Alberto Gordillo, Avenida del Parque. 2/2/3 Puerta A, 13200 Manzanares.

LATIN AMERICA

Dominican Republic: J.M. Morel, Calle 7 edif 45 apto 102, Multis Nuevo la Loteria, La Vega, Rep. Dominicana.

AFRICA

Kenya: Patrick Ndege, PO Box 13627-00100, GPO, Nairobi

Zambia: Kephas Mulenga, PO Box 280168, Kitwe.

ASIA

Japan: Michael, Email: japan.wsm@gmail.com

Australia: Trevor Clarke, Email: wspa.info@yahoo.com.au

This declaration is the basis of our organisation and, because it is also an important historical document dating from the formation of the party in 1904, its original language has been retained.

Object

The establishment of a system of society based upon the common ownership and democratic control of the means and instruments for producing and distributing wealth by and in the interest of the whole community.

Declaration of Principles

The Socialist Party of Great Britain holds:

1. That society as at present constituted is based upon the ownership of the means of living (i.e. land, factories, railways, etc.) by the capitalist or master class, and the consequent enslavement of the working class, by whose labour alone wealth is produced.

2. That in society, therefore, there is an antagonism of interests, manifesting itself as a class struggle between those who possess but do not produce and those who produce but do not possess.

3. That this antagonism can be abolished only by the emancipation of the working class from the domination of the master class, by the conversion into the common property of society of the means of production and distribution, and their democratic control by the whole people.

4. That as in the order of social evolution the working class is the last class to achieve its freedom, the emancipation of the working class will involve the emancipation of all mankind, without distinction of race or sex.

5. That this emancipation must be the work of the working class itself.

6. That as the machinery of government, including the armed forces of the nation, exists only to conserve the monopoly by the capitalist class of the wealth taken from the workers, the working class must organize consciously and politically for the conquest of the powers of government, national and local, in order that this machinery, including these forces, may be converted from an instrument of oppression into the agent of emancipation and the overthrow of privilege, aristocratic and plutocratic.

7. That as all political parties are but the expression of class interests, and as the interest of the working class is diametrically opposed to the interests of all sections of the master class, the party seeking working class emancipation must be hostile to every other party.

8. The Socialist Party of Great Britain, therefore, enters the field of political action determined to wage war against all other political parties, whether alleged labour or avowedly capitalist, and calls upon the members of the working class of this country to muster under its banner to the end that a speedy termination may be wrought to the system which deprives them of the fruits of their labour, and that poverty may give place to comfort, privilege to equality, and slavery to freedom.

Notes